At Work in the Bridal Industry

Poems

Nadell Fishman

At Work in the Bridal Industry

Poems

Nadell Fishman

Plain View Press
P. O. 42255
Austin, TX 78704

plainviewpress.net
sb@plainviewpress.net
512-441-2452

Copyright © 2011 Nadell Fishman. All rights reserved under International and Pan-American Copyright Conventions. No part of this book may be reproduced or distributed in any form or by any means, or stored in a data base or retrieval system, without written permission from the author. All rights, including electronic, are reserved by the author and publisher.

ISBN: 978-1-935514-04-6
Library of Congress Number: 2011934160

Cover art by Carleen Zimbalatti
carleenzimbalatti@yahoo.com

Acknowledgments

Thanks to the following journals and reviews in which earlier versions of these poems appeared:
"Her New Best Friends" in *The Café Review*, Spring 2008; "At Work in the Bridal Industry," "Dorothy Demurs," "The Children of Hamlin Return," "The Town Crier's Last Day on the Job," "Turning 50," "How She Sleeps Now," "Diagnosis," in *Poet Lore*, Spring/Summer 2005, Volume 100, Number ½; "The Last Hours" in *Poet Lore*, Spring/Summer 2006, Volume 101, Number ½; and "Coincidence" in *Hunger Mountain*, Spring 2004.

Thank you dear friends and careful readers: Jane Shore, Judith Chalmer, Charles Barasch, Nicola Morris, Diane Swan, Andrea Gould, Dina L. Wilcox, Victor G. Rodwin, and Tom Absher and members of the Writers' Hotel.

In memory of Susan Bright, founder and editor of Plain View Press, who first championed this manuscript.

*The consolation of imaginary things
is not imaginary consolation.*

P.D. James
The Murder Room

Contents

I

At Work in the Bridal Industry	15
Epithalamion	17
Mah Jongg	18
Turning 50	19
A Woman's Life	20
Coincidence	21
The Meaning of Birds	23
Diagnosis	24
Have You Heard Iris DeMent Sing?	25
How She Sleeps Now	27
Microblast	28
Two Women	29
The Last Hours	30

II

Say Yes to the Dress	35
After the House Falls	37
Unpacking in Purgatory	39
Trompe l'Oeil	40
Her New Best Friends	41
Report From a Far Away Place	43
Girl in the Water	44
How She Sees Herself Reflected in Her Daughter's Eyes	45
Dorothy Demurs	47
The Door That Swings One Way	48
A Daughter Becomes a Cool Customer	50
Lancôme Counter at Macy's	51
Up From All Fours	52
Breathing Lessons	54
Late Family Portrait	56
The Town Crier's Last Day on the Job	57

III

Silent Craft	61
Dreams	62
Ecstasies	63
The Children of Hamlin Return	64
Girl From Brooklyn Discovers Fire	65
To the Checkout Clerk Who Bagged My Tomatoes	67
This Summer the Boy Learns to Whistle	68
Money	69
Coming and Going	70
Vertical Living	71
The 10,000 Steps	73

Notes 75
About the Author 77

for Victor

At Work in the Bridal Industry

"You have to imagine it," my mother says
to the full-grown bride. "You have to imagine
matching ivory pumps, hair up-swirled from your face
(she says this holding that face in her palm)
make-up, manicure, tear drop earrings, veil, bouquet."

She works late nights in the bridal shop
and by the time my father and I
pick her up, she's dead on her feet from lugging
charmeuse, chiffon, faille, organza, and tulle.
"How much do you think a wedding gown weighs?"

she asks, a serious question I can see,
but I'm too light-weight to hold up the copious ton of it,
keep it from dragging. In my child hands
the miniature groom in the waxy tux
bows to the tiny bride, authentic down to her crinolines;

but he might just as soon belt her as bow to her.
It's all play to me, but I suspect even now
my mother's dreams for me include
a wedding dress of ivory georgette
embroidered with silver and crystal beads.

In the framed black and white photograph
she keeps on her dresser,
the train of my mother's white silk crepe gown spreads,
a huge circle pooling on the photographer's studio floor.
It was never myself in the dress I imagined,

but my face in her palm. Veils of illusion,
gossamer, lace, long as a chain reaction.
A language of love my mother speaks
with pins tucked between her lips
to a bride on a pedestal, many brides really,   continued...

reflected and multiplied
inside the world of the triple-hinged,
floor-length mirrors.
"There, there, emotions run high," ma says,
closing the dressing room door, shutting out

the mother-of-the-bride, maid-of-honor
and bridesmaids, but no one's feathers ruffle;
there's frou-frou enough for every hand to caress.
White from veil to heel, the bride preens,
is preened by this total stranger, my mother,

who, from this day forward becomes, until her wedding day,
the bride's very own clothier, handmaid, counselor.
I glimpse these princesses in socks,
skinny flat-chested girls, with nothing to hold up a strapless gown,
so my mother has to bundle the fabric in back

to help them imagine what it will look like
after alterations, or big girls, skin glistening with sweat
after notching up their girdles under the hot lights.
Pet to the sales girls in the shop
where everything's white: chintz love seats,

tasseled lamp shades, faceless mannequins
and disembodied arms displaying
the finest kid gloves, I'm digging pins out of carpet.
Everything has a name: rickrack, sequins, spangles,
as one bride exits and another

steps up to a step collar
or a sweetheart neckline,
marries, boxes up her Tiffany,
while a steady queue of brides
peeps around the crimping, ruching, shirring.

Epithalamion

How hard can it be to love him,
she asks herself as steam
sweats down the shower glass.

How hard can it be to love her
he asks one end of his tie as he knots it
tightly around his neck.

They're old enough to know
better than to believe
there's a perfect word for what they feel.

A wild wind plays the archaic words
of the black robed judge:
it's what the vows don't say.

How can she plight her troth?
She sees herself wifely, toweling off,
growing a hard shell.

And can he vow to forsake all others
with temptations in strappy heels down every street
and his appetite so great?

This story of love, they tell each other
they must reinvent each morning,
as if for a stranger.

Mah Jongg

> *...mixing memory and desire...*
> T.S.Eliot

That summer, we fell in love—
girl love—in a land of women.
Love with sand between its toes,
we showered together,
drank from the same cup.
In the evening, our bodies thrummed
unclenching from the day's heat.

In summer, she lived here,
Beach 29th Street, Rockaway.
In the '60s, the white bungalows
were trimmed dark green,
alive like nobody's business.

Women of all ages on vacation,
in curlers, dangling children,
smoking cigarettes,
playing mah jongg.
Soaps, dots, bams, dragons:
they palmed the cool jade,
clicking the tiles
over an oilcloth covered card table.

She strummed her guitar
and her big-boned voice sang in Yiddish,
sang in American, sang
of desire beginning to flood
my body
poised for womanhood.

Turning 50

Don't mind the number;
for some men and women,
it's a Get Out Of Jail Free card, a portal.
You've known a few of them

newly paired: a grizzled guy
with a fresh face riding his arm.
Don't focus on what optimism isn't.
Find it next to you in bed, that haven

for adulterous dreams, where your husband's body
still fits yours and rolls synchronously
into the settling night.
Mind the whiskers, yours,

and when you search your face in the mirror
don't faint when you see your mother's face
replace it; they said it would; and they said
your kid's childhood would go by in an instant

and that was true, too.
Mind the distance between you
and that twenty-three year old who runs around
inside you, that part of your better self,

and not because she didn't age.
Whatever optimism is, that girl knows,
she defined it for you long ago.
Go to her now, not as a supplicant

but as the legs, Sweetheart,
carrying you both into the future.

A Woman's Life

None of the other family members remember it now,
how we arrived home late one evening and Grandma—

short and stout in her 80s, who we'd left playing solo
Gin Rummy and reading her *Jewish Daily Forward*,

and who had the strength of the 7 Santini Brothers Movers—
had rearranged my mother's living room furniture.

Now I can see the views my mother saw, the brand new vistas
from the black and silver-threaded sectional sofa,

wing chair, and piano bench through the picture window
as a design rebuke of a daughter-in-law my grandmother believed

wasn't good enough to marry her eldest American son
for she'd already picked out a meek girl to be his bride.

In Queens where she walked a careful hobble up
one broken cement sidewalk and down the other,

a caged myna whistled its lascivious mimicry
at her from the porch of the dark red house opposite ours.

And she never saw a single face she knew
after she'd already lived three lifetimes

in Poland, Ukraine and Belarus—
America with its foreign food and foreign language

was far from the country she fled with its pogroms, and poverty,
and a husband and two sons she would never see again.

Coincidence

There was the slim notion,
illuminated now,
that a glance
in the right direction
a woman and a man

passing on stairs,
in a dingy stairwell,
with a rough wooden railing,
and steep, worn treads,
might be the barely

perceptible filament
from which future
life dangles. It wasn't
the stairway to heaven.
I'd already traveled

three hundred miles north,
and still going up,
I could see my breath indoors.
I was free.
I could go anywhere.

I climbed as
you descended.
I noticed your hatless
head, your dark
curls on that frigid

February day.
Down a step, you
turned below me
and our eyes met.

continued...

Over the years,
when we tell it,
a detail is left out,
or a new one pops up,
for instance,

that I stopped
after you'd passed,
and looked back again
because you'd surprised me
into wanting everything,

the whole fairy story,
a happy ending
with a white dress and rings
and you, for better
or for worse.

The Meaning of Birds

In moving meditation, she awakens her spine,
that armature, as never before, easing flesh, soothing muscle.
Her hands float up as if to touch her startled face.

She's sad because the dog died, the cat's disappeared,
and the girl, now grown, has moved away.
In moving meditation, she awakens her spine.

In sleep her husband looks well and his body moves
as if preparing for flight.
Her hands float up as if to touch her startled face.

That morning she dreams of birds.
A cockatiel points the way—forward or back—she doesn't know.
In moving meditation, she awakens her spine.

In the dream's logic the bird lives in its cage,
exotic feathers luminous white, wings outstretched.
Her hands float up as if to touch her startled face.

Three lustrous plumes issue from its crown. It's lonely
without the child, the dog, the cat and after she speaks of it,
in moving meditation, she awakens her spine.
Her hands float up as if to touch her startled face.

Diagnosis

The first few answers leap
    into their squares; your mind limber,
        flexed as fingers.

The brain on an overhead projector is gray,
    nothing like a crossword puzzle,
        with all its parts labeled black.

It's the left side of his body that slows
    its pace and the answer means
        the part of the brain, black substance,

in 14 letters, where his cells
    cease to fire. Seven, eight and nine across
        are giveaways:

six letters for a winter sport, four for shut noisily,
    six for Aloha state;
        but you're no good at games

and competitive at the same time:
    there must be a word for that.
        7 letters for that brainy elixir

that commands the body to move—now.
    Then the door slams and you're skiing in Hawaii.
        You should always use a pencil

with a good eraser. Now the answers to eleven, twelve and
    thirteen across elude you, run just ahead of you
        as you swipe at them

left, right, left again. Across and across, down, down,
    and down. 12 letters for what's happening
        to his hand trembling in air.

Have You Heard Iris DeMent Sing?

I'm trying to convince my husband
to rock with me on the porch, after all
it's as summer as it's going to be
this far north, the wooden runners so green
the rockers practically weep.
So I think I'll try out
this CD I bought to his surprise
since I'm hardly ever the one
who purchases music in this house
but I'd heard this woman's voice
on the radio and something
about the way her sound
almost hurt me, not what she sang,
but how. I think it may be
just what we need to wind through
the tree tops, the rockers,
and the two of us
staring into each other's eyes
on a do-nothing
summer day
when I know full well he'd rather
be limbing trees, square
in the buzz of his chainsaw,
but he's here listening
to this woman whose voice confuses
my ear then in the last possible breath
blows its heat over me,
and just as we settle into a rhythm,
our rockers chasing each other's
downbeat round the planks,
an inchworm, laboriously
stitches its way
down one side of a rocker
while another makes its way
up from the bottom

continued...

of the same curvy rocker.
They're looping themselves toward,
each other, when Iris sings,
over what must be her ear to ear smile,
"It's hotter than Mojave in my heart,"
and my husband's hooked on Iris
in less time than it took me
to enjoy a dry Martini
with as many olives as fit
on a toothpick, and the inchworms
press onward to the one
who might be its mate.

How She Sleeps Now

In her dream of the snake
there is a cowboy in a ten-gallon hat
who promises with imprudent calm,
given the situation,
he will nail the sucker with his first shot,
no problem.

She tells it to her husband in the banality
of morning, for he's asked how she slept
and all the nights of their years
are silent against this new terror
that rattles her and glares back at them
from the future.

Only now has she begun to share her bed
with an intractable animal
that takes and takes and takes from him,
its weight pressing down
so when he walks, he drags a leg.

They'll have a laying on of hands,
a curative spring,
slow stiffening of days.
If only she might decipher what the snake knows,
its ancient message
that no cowboy twirling a revolver
can overpower.

Shot after misfired shot
brings her upright in bed.
She looks back at her love reclining,
up on one elbow
a sleep smile on his face,
a snake coiled at his feet.

Microblast

When he left, no one heard
crashing sounds around her.
This went on for some time.
When the trees began to fly
that day of night,
she took it as a sign
the sounds, external now,
as 40-foot pines bounced
off the roof and pounded cars
in the drive. Outside the windows
everything whipped by unhinged,
untethered, unmoored, as if in the next moment
the house might lift off and she'd ride
the eye, another Dorothy exiting Kansas
the hard way. How perfectly
the outside mirrored the crazy way
she felt inside, knowing
she'd have to leave home.
When silence finally dropped,
neighbors came with chainsaws
that buzzed for hours,
jaws of life come to free her.
Hardwoods and soft woods down,
mammoths decomposing where they fell.

Two Women

Grief is immeasurable,
a continuously filling well.
Who would wish to claim
her grief is greater?
That woman
whose husband drops
dead at the dinner table
one evening, a Tuesday, say,
when they've been eating leftovers
out of Chinese takeout cartons
and he's just brought over and set down
on the bare table, his glass, quarter full
of amber liquid, mid-thought, words poised,
half said, that woman's grief
or that other woman,
the one whose husband leaves her
after they've been together for 25 years,
raised a daughter,
built a home,
leaves her for another woman,
and says to her before he leaves
as if to bring down whole
upon her head the sky,
I can't imagine
living the rest of my life
without joy.

The Last Hours

In the last hours
of their union
she said their names
out loud, over and over,
one tone tumbling into another.
She said their first names
the way friends said them
as one word, meaning
one particular life.

She said his distinguished middle
and family names,
which she'd never taken
yet which were hers,
and the name of her father,
which was hers still.
She saw the word *family*
erased from its place
across a blue sky.

She saw their daughter,
the child they'd made
together, untether,
spiral away from them.
She saw the look
on some friends' faces, the look
that showed whose side they took,
the reasons why
they must turn and leave.

She saw the legal documents'
red arrows spearing the lines
where her signature
and his signature once fixed
would sever their union
just like that—gone.

She removed his photograph
from a drawer,
lay down on their bed
and cupped a hand
over one small breast
as he had so often done,
while he looked on
without a word.

Say Yes to the Dress

I married in a plain white blouse and skirt
with a little Mexican embroidery around hem
and sleeve. It said *bad planning* on my part,
it said *lack of funds* that would dog my life.

It was a Wednesday and I'd worked all day.
After the ceremony in our living room,
our small party drove to the restaurant country inn,
where we'd made a reservation, but it was closed.

The women watching *Say Yes to the Dress*
hurl accusations at a bride-to-be's father (the wallet),
who invited him anyway; what does he know
about style, the strapless, and slenderizing?

They're riveted to the beauty: a bride
in the perfect dress, Cinderella, finally marrying,
as she was meant to be from the beginning in the '50s
at the height of the dream when hair was big
and bouffi, and a gown's silk went on for miles.

Today, you can say *yes* to a dress
off the rack for $100 at David's
and save your parents' retirement, but if they insist,
go straight to Vera Wang at Kleinfeld's, NYC.

I sat behind Suzanne's friends on the train one day
as they discussed her dress. I don't know who she is,
but I know her dress is a giant cream puff
that cost a bundle, so what's a girl to do,

Suzanne bought it its own seat on the plane
to travel east to their wedding—"*Pull out the stopper,
let's have a whopper. But get me to the church on time.*"
I wonder where that dress is now.

continued...

When she was 19, my daughter said *yes*
to an ivory strapless so form-fitting
she had to wear a one-piece seamless undergarment
to fuse body and dress together.

The following month, my sister said *yes* for a third time
to an antique silk gown she says she'll dye
and hope to wear again
because it isn't the dress's fault.

That same summer, my niece said *yes*
to a traditional wedding with great *hors d'oeuvres*.
She looked gaunt in her fitted bodice
and machine-made lace veil.

At her ceremony on a beach the bridal party
wore flip flops below gowns and tuxes.
Hers seems to be the statistical anomaly;
well, and why not, she's such a pretty girl.

Mine began with the shuttered restaurant.
We'd left the reservation on an answering machine,
as we'd done before, and never thought to confirm,
but it was off-season.

The owner chef came to the door of the darkened house
in his boxers. He looked sad and said if he'd had any food
in his refrigerator, he'd have cooked us
our wedding meal.

After the House Falls

She drinks alone.
Pours herself
a tall glass of grief
and slowly drinks
until the edges blur.

They try to console her
with aphorisms. They say
life turns on a dime.
There aren't dimes enough,
she knows, to buy back

for her that life.
She says there's a fist
in her chest
and when it flexes
she can't breathe.

But no one's there
to hear this.
Time heals all things
they say, but she picks that scab,
imagines it might occupy her

for the rest of her life.
She's weak. She's lost her grip.
They tell her *enough is enough.*
What is enough of nothing,
she wonders.

Impulsively, she phones him
knowing all she'll get
will be his voice machine
saying *I'm not here.*
Leave a message,

continued...

and a chasm opens up
between the end of his voice
and where she stands. It is so long,
so wide, she believes she will hear
this silence between them forever.

Unpacking in Purgatory

She does it alone.
That's one of the tortures.
Packing was a blazing red hell,
packing after 19 years

but she called in the troops,
the reinforcements
and they came
with bad backs in old trucks

scant time and good gossip.
They took instruction,
whispered in corners,
made their own decisions,

wrapped glass
in inky newspaper,
in the funnies,
filled 30-gallon Hefty's

and Seagram's cartons.
They stopped asking;
she couldn't decide—
this vase, that cup—

couldn't imagine
their things cramped in a small
walk up apartment,
living without him.

Trompe l'Oeil

When half the contents
of her elegant Victorian crowds her porch,

she begins to fathom the depths of love
object by misplaced object.

She takes to drink, smokes Marlboros,
grows thin as a dark reed

until the porch is vacated, and the emptiness
inside rearranges itself.

Lucky furniture doesn't bleed.
Lucky the wedding crystal

doesn't shatter from grief.
The sturdy Larkin desk

built to last 100 years;
a wavery mirror, she couldn't rely on

to tell her what it saw;
the best of their jazz collection

still in jackets; bric-a-brac packed
and corded for hauling.

Ten years of waking
beside the warm flesh of another

come down to who will take possession
of the two-cup Pyrex measure.

Her New Best Friends

The *I Ching* and a dildo arrive
in separate brown packages.
They're chatting her up
in their foreign languages

as she tears through stapled seams.
What, you ask,
is she doing with her life?
You roll your eyes and decide

you have nothing in common with her.
She must be desperate,
but you're wrong.
It's only her turn

to be a student of emptiness,
that's her field now
and she's romping through high grass
each new friend under an arm.

She'll toss the coins.
She'll smell her own juices.
You're disgusted.
Who wants to know

about the real life
of a woman alone,
a woman who sports
with a neon pink gel dildo

she met on the Internet.
The coins say *decreasing and increasing.*
Being full and being empty.
These take place in accord with the conditions

continued...

of time. Time, they tell her, you need it,
it's a healer and in time you'll forget.
In the meantime, be patient,
count on your friends and learn to love yourself.

Report From a Far Away Place

Ambushed, I caught myself in the glass of a photograph
I'd innocently stopped on the staircase to adjust.

My grim face mirrored over my seated family smiling back at me.
Or I'd hear my once-married voice on the message machine

because I inadvertently pressed the wrong button.
I got into my car and drove fast through slush and muddy snow

to the nearest luggage store, where I purchased six red nesting
suitcases, three on wheels, and placed them—separately—

in the middle of the living room, so I'd have to walk around them,
contemplate their various sizes and shapes. The largest

could wheel away a small standing child, while the smallest
folded in on itself securing little plastic bottles that were empty.

I assessed their many inner and outer zippered compartments
where I might lose a gold ring, for instance, or stow a sheaf

of signed documents, and forced myself to imagine one open
on my bed, half-packed with thin, colorful summer clothing,

as if a small welcome note on a pillow in a beachside cabana
in the Caribbean had my name on it; or myself ensnaring

the largest valise off carousel number 4 or 7 at JFK after a trip
to a place I never before saw myself,

a place where the moment before my departure,
my imagination just ends, and the Earth, all broken

into countries with airports and people and languages,
begins and I am fearless.

Girl in the Water

Her daughter enters the water, her sunburnt face
a worrisome map her mother studies.
The lake made rough by motorboats
mystifies a mother's anxious eye that watches
from the dock, her hand blocking the sun's glare.
The water is a silent conduit between them.
It laps her twenty-year-old body
and what she imagines are its imperfections.
It whirls her in its arms, raises her up
for a moment, then pulls her under,
a malevolent hand, while her mother
holds her breath until the dyed blonde hair bobs.
The girl's head swivels around, disoriented
from being under water, but the surface, too,
is strange: there her mother is alone, her father
no longer a man either one trusts.
And what endures is not the low sun
obliterating everything in its path,
nor the circle of flames
that water cannot extinguish
but her mother's steadfast eyes
that keep her girl in sight.

How She Sees Herself Reflected in Her Daughter's Eyes

What's her body saying?
Have you thought about that

while you're chattering on
and her feet point in the direction

of leaving? You're stringing your sentences together,
while italicized words introduced

by a little background clarinet
sound in your head; they say: *pinched toes,*

cucumber mask, vodka.
She's getting into a car

(mmm nice car)
and since this is your fantasy

it's a red convertible
and the top's down

because while you stand in winter,
layered in silk underwear and woolies,

the sun is enthralled with her.
You think she'll drive this car

to New York City or Montreal *(oh la la)*
where she'll find a parking space

outside an apartment building.
Now there's a key in her pocket.

Now her name's over a mailbox.
In the elevator—you can feel the lift

continued...

in your stomach though you stand perfectly still—
she knows what floor to press.

Anytime she jolts you out of this state,
her teeth all in it, she'll smile

(*sunglasses, skipped meals,
empty house*) but don't mistake that for a sign

of her attentiveness. She can talk to you
a little and turning, continue

in the direction in which she moved
all the while you were missing her.

Dorothy Demurs

Dorothy's decided that Oz suits her.
All that living color, who's surprised?
She digs in; won't click her heels.
For certain, that's no tin man
she's curled up with, either.
At the second-hand store, Dorothy trades in
her gingham frock. Black's her color.

Too bad about those slippers—
Now she's wearing suede knee-high boots,
a star tattoo above her belly button,
and a diamond pierces her nose.
Her Uncle Henry and I always say,
There's no place like home,
but Dorothy's young

she's got the wanderlust.
Who am I to say? I had it, too,
hitchhiked my way up and down
dirt roads all over the USA
and let me tell you, Kansas
is a state of mind.
We sent out the flying monkeys

to no avail, flamed *Surrender, Dorothy*
across the daytime sky.
My mother worried herself sick
when I left home. In truth, it took a twister
to bring me back. Now the farm's gone,
some days I'm in my own way
and miss her something fierce.

The Door That Swings One Way

The door that swings one way
emits a thin, unpredictable
shaft of light

and sounds that buzz in
now and then
and there are two people

who live their lives
within sight of the door:
they are neither

protagonist
nor antagonist;
yet they are blind,

deaf and unable,
unwilling to allow
that the light or the sound

might have something to do
with them. They might be
on the same side

of the door. They might
watch it swing away.
They might be an inch

from its farthest arc,
both on the other side,
and feel the air rushing past;

therefore, they never see
what is framed in the thin column of light,
never hear what might be uttered.

His were the shaky hands
that caught her slipping wet into life, or to clarify,
they are father and daughter.

Their past goes on without them
in a particular house. Their past
that swings one way and comes to stillness.

A Daughter Becomes a Cool Customer

When that moment came after 16 hours of pacing
and climbing the stairs, and the midwife said:
We're going to the hospital
unless something happens pretty soon,
torque took over all the workings of my body
such as is not known in the man-made world.
One hour later you were lying on my belly.
I know, how embarrassing
and who really cares anyway,
but in that hour, my body learned
what it would never have need of again
and yet that information, of muscles in concert,
of blood and shit and grunts working together,
and the searing tearing of flesh willingly giving way
to pass you out into the world
~surely there are uses for such knowledge.
Hasn't it lodged in my brain matter?
Isn't its phantom rippling through my body now
when I hear your cold and distant voice
over the cell phone at my ear,
speaking to me as if I were a stranger,
or with even less regard? And my body,
recognizing this foreign knot in my gut,
wants to expel it,
and, a little kick of ghostly pain
undulates through me without resolution.

Lancôme Counter at Macy's

Her black lab coat swishes,
shiny Rayon against Rayon.
Long sleeves cover up
her own colorful tattoos,
as she brushes the shimmery powder
onto the eyelid of an older—older
by far than she—coiffed woman
seated elegantly before her
on a swivel stool.

They look into each other's eyes,
breathe each other's breath,
touch knees. How long
has she ministered to this customer
in the middle of Macy's main floor?
Unbeknownst to her, I'm hiding behind a mirror,
spying, while a woman nearby tries on too pointy
patent shoes, and another drags a crabby child
by her arm.

The young "expert" plies her art
to the woman's already lovely face,
I can see, tilted toward her
in their shared idea of beauty,
achieving it on this madonna, madam, ma'am
and then as if felt
or seen by a third eye,
my daughter turns her rapturous face to me
and smiles.

Up From All Fours

> *What if the Hokey Pokey*
> *really is what it's all about?*
> Restaurant Graffiti

First we had opposable thumbs
and from there it was just a *left arm in*,
a *right arm out*—to the wheel
and then the Winchester.
It wasn't the wild wild West

when my Bubbe arrived green
off the boat waving at Lady Liberty;
it was the *Cyclone* at Coney Island
that curled her toes.
She wanted to live with her heart

joyfully in her throat.
The Troika was a dangerous step
she'd left behind.
Everyone in a circle, called Mrs. Casson
my third grade teacher, bless her 1950s

blonde beehive. We'd clomp to formation.
Future moms and dads, model citizens
of the world—we'd quake, and shake it all about.
We've been dancing in circles
as far back as recorded history goes,

even the dog chases his tail.
My sister's favorite saying is
Chicken Little was right.
Meanwhile the planet warms,
and yellow fever and malaria pack their bags

for the move north.
I can't say exactly why I turn myself
day in and day out,
but I noticed right away
the day when no one held hands.

Breathing Lessons

At 74, my father had to learn to breathe.
His emerging breath would not sustain
the many notes he yearned to sing.

So he went to school
to learn a cantor's breath,
to sing the cantor's song.

He learned breathing isn't the action
of a slight wind that stirs
stale air, a few chest high cups

that whistle their way out
but another practice altogether:
a bellows waking; the bowl of a belly

filling, breath spiraling.
Many hours I've listened
to my father's instructive breath,

a cantor's prayerful song,
telling and retelling the story
of the children of Abraham,

the begetting, the betrayals, all manner
of manna from heaven, and oh, the wandering.
When a big man takes a breath,

the sound he sings from the back of a sanctuary
precedes him, past aisles and aisles
of head-covered men and women,

past his own Brooklyn youth
past the printer's ink and type,
years of back-stiffening, eye-blinding work.

He coaxes his breath
up through his body's cellular stories,
modulates the exit of breath and beatific sound.

Late Family Portrait

A nurse straightens the last fold of sheet
before picking up the phone.
He's sleeping, she tells us long distance,
I just put him to bed. She's his little mother now,
wisps of gray hair straying from her bun.
Her accented English, though
not the Russian-Yiddish inflection
of that first mother's tongue,
thickly blankets her eighty-year old son.
*It seems the sky is raining the other shoe
just now.* Far from home, a daughter
imagines dangers insidious
as staph, imagines
her mother's wordless pacing,
how she holds her own hands
after the table is set,
how the quiet she loathes
booms throughout the house.
You must pull yourself together, Father.
You must straighten your tie.
What does your wristwatch say?
My sister and I distract our mother.
We're waiting for you to sing
our thanks to God and break our bread.

The Town Crier's Last Day on the Job

Mom's hearing is shot, so the volume's
turned way up to drown out the wailing
baby downstairs. We're watching daytime TV;
invited Barbara Walters and her friends
into a real living room, complete
with hair of a dog, to buffer conversations
we're too shy to have together.
Other family members hide out
at the bitter end of noise.
Outside, cement absorbs the unusual
April heat, the living room windows
wide open. After the springtime
scent of armpits, the pine scent
of fine wooden floors,
the lemon scent of toilet bowls,
Barbara is back with a vengeance.
From the shimmering screen, the TV women
exalt in the repetition of a new play's title:
The Vagina Monologues, they blush and giggle.
Vagina's three syllables sandwiched
between commercials. *Vagina* singing,
escaping through the fine mesh squares of screening.
Vagina working its magic
on the mortified face of my father,
stepping lightly into the living room.
We break for a few words
from our sponsor, too stunned to speak.
What's been broken is our taboo.
All of us standing around the living room
rendered naked by the fact of *that* word
smiling everywhere.

Silent Craft

Kayak adrift. This far
from everyone on shore, and right
in the middle of the pond,
she is nearly face to beak
with a loon. Through dark pond nights
she hears them echoing,
foretelling the coming day;
and it arrives on the tail end
of the banner of their various calls:
mate, I'm here waiting for you;
young ones, I'm here waiting for you to fly;
fish, I'm here waiting to pounce on you;
and danger, the humans are within
a couple of wing spans.
The large, dark head, used to the scream
of motor boats passing,
looks up at her silence.
The loon dips its beak
into the mirror of pond water
and is gone. She'll paddle her wavy way
back to the grassy inlet,
back to the smoky grill
that signals how her ancestors
once ate after the kill,
after the gathering of berries,
flowers, tubers and roots.
She travels a long way back.
Inside the cabin she encounters love
with the man who turns her sun-browned body,
and her vestige of sadness,
toward him.

Dreams

She hadn't been touched
by a man's hands, lips, tongue,
since his year of living dangerously
left her stupefied in an overstuffed chair,
and took him to another's bed.
There she was in winter,
her little dog pressed against her back
in the too-large bed, knees to chest,
padded in flannel.
In a fairy tale, vines might have
knotted their wiry fingers,
enveloping her house on its piney lot.

By the time summer came around again
she'd uncurled, stretched herself
into the center of her new queen-sized bed.
The dog snored lightly,
running in his sleep. Nothing
in her sounding would wake him
from his dream of chasing the gray squirrel
teasing and chattering at him from a high branch.

Ecstasies

The Sangiovese goes to her knees.
Her cheeks blaze up
and there's a man; that's how they meet.

    On their walks, her little dog
    sniffs a dry, brown branch.
    Nose and singular object commune.

Long after the meal, there's a man,
the same man, who took her full measure
from the other side of that dinner table.

    Face full into the wind as if setting sail,
    the dog braces his body. Is this his delight,
    the barrage of scents that ripple over his short snout?

The man's kisses walk her backwards
to her high bed where no man has yet
wrapped her body in his.

    Ecstatic asleep and awake,
    the curlicue of a white dog
    levitates from tip to tail.

She wakes in the man's arms again and again.
For once it seems time replenishes
what it steals.

The Children of Hamlin Return

Disgorged, as from a great belch in the mountain
back, back, back they came
in waves of eager faces: some deep
in five o'clock shadow, some swollen
with pregnant bellies.

They returned hungry for their lives as children:
magic of the replenishing refrigerator,
clean folded clothes,
silvery hologram of the VISA card,
their parents' open arms.

But meanwhile Hamlin is transformed
with landscaping, pergolas,
espaliered apple trees and trellises
climbing the walls of houses
reshaping themselves with bay windows,

conservatories, porticoes. Winnebagos
in their drives. Twin beds,
shelves of soccer trophies, and repainted nurseries morph
into home offices with PCs
or gyms with rowing machines and Stairmasters.

From treadmills, parents greet their dismayed children:
how their parents' lives have moved on after so many years
without children at home! Legions of moms and dads
reconcile their loss with relief,
remember each other, themselves.

Girl From Brooklyn Discovers Fire

Once, camp meant summers spent
six girls to a tent, sleeping on narrow cots
and scratching arms and legs bloody
from mosquito bites. In mid-life,
alone, camp on Shadow Lake
is a cottage in August. She pays the rent
and it's unseasonably cold; loons call
over the mist rising and shadows do fall
from the other side of the lake.
She shivers under an assortment
of Army blankets, coverlets and rag tag quilts.
By morning her joints complain
and she must build a fire
in the small camp stove.
She zips herself into gray fleece,
pulls up her socks.
Camp is well stocked for weather,
but here there's *arts & crafts* before breakfast,
or breakfast in the fog of her own breath.
She fashions donuts
out of full sheets of newspaper,
stacked and yellowing,
and when there's a stash,
she assembles the pyre.
In the cold beside the water,
she thinks *my life depends on fire.*
A cry beats its wings through the air
as if up from her depths.
She strikes a match
and several corners of the *Times* catch.
The dry kindling blazes up,
eventually, she settles a log
onto the coals; the fire takes the log.

continued...

Through the morning she feeds the fire
and slowly the house and her body
warm.

To the Checkout Clerk Who Bagged My Tomatoes

Boy who barely reaches the top of the cash register,
boy whose smooth cheeks flush red

when we make eye contact, what do you know
of produce except what's good on a burger.

Boy with red bitten fingernails and a cowlick that won't quit,
student of a harried supervisor's slap-dash instructions,

I stand by and watch as you slide peaches in syrup
clanging against each other, send soup cans sloshing,

a lone baby eggplant bruises a deeper purple,
noodles rattle in their nests.

I thought I'd seen audacity until you toss my tomatoes,
into my canvas bag and then with a slight curl

of your lip, the five pounds of organic potatoes,
the concentrated orange juice at the end of its journey

all the way from Florida, the twin California melons
with names I can't pronounce. Your act

is the indelicate catch and hurl of a demented juggler
doing the up and over: your eyes fix on mine,

my hands reach for the bag, inches
from your face, my hands so near applause.

This Summer the Boy Learns to Whistle

At almost 16, he's taller than I am
and I do resent having to look up
to talk to this son of my lover.
Now he resembles his mother: all angles and dark curls.
A cousin says *Caravaggio would have painted him.*
When I helped him parse *Gatsby* for tenth-grade English
it forged our friendship.
He's teaching himself to whistle.
I never learned and admire his gumption.
His is the practice-whistle in the '50s TV cartoon
in which a demure bird was to whistle
when danger was near, but it was his enemy, the cat,
who told him and stuffed his mouth full of crackers.
His father, a skilled whistler, registers his dismay
over the whole enterprise.
He's had nothing to complain about all summer:
He's so helpful, he keeps telling me
but this half-whistling is less endearing
than his son's sometimes-manly sounds
that crack willy-nilly along the ridge
of his almost abandoned child's voice—
the near-whistling is more than
his father's equilibrium can bear,
each attempt eliciting its accompaniment of groans,
until one day, his persistence pays off
and from somewhere in the house we hear
the first sure soaring notes of his glissando.

Money

> *...that clinking, clanking sound
> can make the world go round.*
>   Kander & Ebb

Outside the automatic doors of the Superette,
on Broadway, he wobbles to keep warm, a skeleton of a man
in black, small enough to be a child except for his face.
A well-dressed woman retraces her steps, extends a dollar bill.
He blesses her, says he'll eat today.

Money plays tricks on me, has done so all my life.
In my pocket it feels so good; I want to absorb its heat,
spread it out to cushion my feet. It celebrates its own holiday,
but the math I learned in school didn't teach me
how to make it multiply.

The man has rheumy eyes. I know this because
I look directly into them as I walk by.
If my head swims from aromas wafting around us
from the corner's halal quick lunch cart,
then his must swoon.

When we make eye contact,
mine say to the man in front of the grocery store,
there's nothing in my pockets for either of us.
But he wouldn't believe me,
not in this neighborhood,

not with the disguise I wear, brown suede coat
tall leather boots, not until there's a bill
on the sidewalk between us.
Who will be first to dive down on the ground,
and who will curse the other?

Coming and Going

A walk in the park is
          just a walk in the park, whatever else

it may once have been. On Riverside,
          she navigates the treacherous cobbles.

Every variety of dog with its doppelganger
          at the other end of the leash

alternately barks or snarls at her.
          She takes each *Grrrr, Arf, Yip*

for a salutation: both coming and going.
          Who she is now, even to herself

is a mystery, and if she could speak
          the droopy-eyed dog

who looks up from her business
          on account of her owner's command

Thelma, say goodbye, might be the oracle
          who chooses not to say, might say more.

Everyone is going quickly somewhere.
          She is going there too,

slowly, going there deliberately,
          at a suspicious pace,

she gathers from the looks on the park bench
          sitters' faces. As they say back home:

she is "from away,"
          though she was once "from here."

Vertical Living

All on one floor, it used to be
in and out were a matter of a few footsteps:
in a storm door; out a screen door.
I could straddle my indoor
outdoor worlds and the life
on either side was mine.
But, in vertical living there are doormen.
I call them by their first names:
Robert, Guililat, Asbenh, Pedro.
They already know everything
about me: who comes, who goes,
my laundry (I send it out),
my meals (I bring them in).
Every day, I thank a doorman
for the door he opens to let me in,
let me out. Every evening,
I wish him good night,
the man down there working
while I sleep! Twelve stories up, I wait
for the ancient elevator to bump
into place while French or Russian conversations
and cooking smells waft all around me.
I submit to this faceless, touchless intimacy,
except for accidental elbows
and shoulders in a crowded lift.
It's communal this vertical life
in the neutralizing elevator and lobby
without all the fussiness
of sharing. But what's an elevator
to a dog used to running wild
in deep snow, used to no sound
but the sound of woods?
He howls
and we humans eagerly translate

continued...

his utterances: some believe
them to be dark, malevolent;
others hear his assent
and rejoice.

The 10,000 Steps

Here, they don't call it a hike
when you walk down York,
down Lexington, down Park,
down Madison in the wind-wallopping
rain, your umbrella turning
inside out and back again
from 86th Street to 34th.
Beside me my sister from out-of-town
strides in long-legged steps,
and she's smiling
into the biting wind.
Stranger in a strange place,
mine is the old story:
the displaced homemaker
starting out late in life,
starting a new life.
We're walking for our health,
you could say, no schedule to bind us,
rush us, but the icy wind.
We walk to find the city in ourselves,
again, or I do and she accompanies me
on my search: tugboat to my barge.
I slow my pace and smile
too much, but I'm a native
and I don't need a pedometer
to tell me how many steps I took
to get here.

Notes

"At Work in the Bridal Industry" is for Rhoda Fishman.

The epigraph to "Mah Jongg" "…mixing memory and desire…" is from "The Waste Land" by T.S.Eliot. The poem is for Sheryl Talbot Silvers.

Say Yes to the Dress is the name of a TV show on TLC; the lyric quoted: "Pull out the stopper, let's have a whopper. But get me to the church on time!" is from "Get Me To The Church On Time," *My Fair Lady* by Lerner & Loewe. The poem is for Jane Shore.

"Trompe l'Oeil" is for Dianne Maccario.

"Lancôme Counter at Macy's" is for Lilian F. Kline.

"Breathing Lessons" is for Samuel Fishman.

"This Summer the Boy Learns to Whistle" is for Aaron H. Rodwin.

The epigraph to "Money" "…that clinking, clanking sound can make the world go round" is from "Money, Money" from *Cabaret* by Kander & Ebb.

"The 10,000 Steps" is for Dina L. Wilcox.

About the Author

Nadell Fishman's first collection of poems, *Drive*, was published in 2001. Her work has appeared in journals and reviews, including *Hunger Mountain*, *Poet Lore* and *Café Review*. Ms. Fishman has been on the faculty of the B.A. program of Union Institute & University for more than 16 years. She lives in Manhattan with her husband, Victor Rodwin and their Westie, Boo Radley.